World Famous Sauces and Dressings Cookbook: Big Brand Secret Recipes Revealed

Table of Contents

A1 Sauce 4

Arby's Barbecue Sauce 5

Arby's Horsey Sauce 6

Benihana Magic Mustard Sauce 7

Benihana Ginger Salad Dressing 8

Benning's Hot Bacon Dressing 9

Good Season's Italian Dressing 10

Heinz 57 Sauce 11

Hidden Valley Ranch Dressing 12

Kraft Thousand Island Dressing 13

Little Caesar's Crazy Sauce 14

McDonald's Big Mac Sauce 15

McDonald's Honey Mustard Sauce 16

McDonald's Hot Mustard Sauce 17

McDonald's Sweet and Sour Sauce 18

Olive Garden House Dressing 19

Papa John's Garlic Sauce 20

Pizza Hut Creamy Italian Dressing 21

Ponderosa's Steak Sauce 22

Red Lobster Tartar Sauce 23

Sbarro sauce 24

Taco Bell Green Sauce 25

Taco Bell Hot Sauce 26

T.G.I. Friday's Soy Dressing 27

Wicker's BBQ Sauce 28

A1 Sauce

Ingredients:

- ½ C 2 T Ketchup
- 1 T yellow mustard
- 1 T Worcestershire sauce
- 2 ¼ C apple cider vinegar
- 1 T lemon juice
- ¼ tsp salt and pepper

Directions:

I. Mic everything together, and you can adjust the lemon juice to taste

II. Store in a mason jar or plastic container with squeeze top

Arby's Barbecue Sauce

Ingredients:

- 1 C ketchup
- 2 tsp water
- ¼ tsp garlic powder
- ¼ tsp onion powder
- ¼ tsp pepper
- ¼ tsp salt
- ½ tsp tabasco pepper sauce

Directions:

I. Add everything together in a saucepan and let heat over medium to low heat but be sure to stir constantly
II. Bring to a quick boil, but no more than 6-8 minutes
III. Remove from heat and let cool
IV. Store in air tight container in the fridge

Arby's Horsey Sauce

Ingredients:

- 1 C mayo
- 1 T sugar
- ¼ C + 2 T horseradish
- ¼ tsp salt

Directions:

I. In a bowl stir everything together, you want to make sure it's well blended and store in the fridge in an air tight container for about an hour at least before using

Benihana Magic Mustard Sauce

Ingredients:

- 1 T toasted sesame seeds, crushed
- 3 T dry mustard
- 2 T hot water
- ¾ C soy sauce
- ¼ T minced garlic
- 3 T heavy cream

Directions:

I. Mix the mustard and water in a mixing bowl until pasty.
II. Blend the paste, seeds, soy sauce and garlic
III. Blend high for one minute, pour back into a bowl and stir in the whipped cream

Benihana Ginger Salad Dressing

Ingredients:

- ½ C minced onion
- ½ C peanut oil
- 1/3 C rice vinegar
- 2 T water
- 2 T minced fresh ginger
- 2 T minced celery
- 2 T ketchup
- 4 tsp soy sauce
- 2 tsp sugar
- 2 tsp lemon juice
- ½ tsp minced garlic
- ½ tsp salt
- ¼ tsp pepper

Directions:

I. Blend everything in your blender or food processor for 30 seconds on high, you want the ginger pureed

II. Chill in fridge

Benning's Hot Bacon Dressing

Ingredients:

- ¼ lbs. diced red onion
- 2 C water
- ½ C honey
- ½ C red wine vinegar
- 2 T Dijon mustard
- 1 ½ T cornstarch
- 1 T tabasco sauce

Directions:

I. Start with the bacon grease in a skillet over heat, and add the onions, you want to sauté them
II. In a separate bowl add the water, honey pepper and red wine vinegar
III. Wish the ingredients together
IV. Add the cornstarch, now in the skillet, add the Dijon, and stir with the onions
V. Add the mix to the skillet and thicken, it will get to a boil (or at least you want it too)
VI. Store in fridge in air tight container

Good Season's Italian Dressing

Ingredients:

Dry mix

- 1 T garlic salt
- 1 T onion powder
- 1 T sugar
- 2 T oregano
- 1 tsp pepper
- ¼ tsp. thyme
- 1 tsp basil
- 1 T parsley
- ¼ tsp celery salt
- 2 T salt

Dressing

- ¼ C cider vinegar
- 2/3 C olive oil
- 2 T water
- 2 T dry mix

Directions:

I. Combine all the dry ingredients together and store in air tight container
II. Add all the dressing ingredients into a mason jar and add lid, shake well

Heinz 57 Sauce

Ingredients:

- 1 T ketchup
- 1 ¼ tsp Worcestershire sauce
- ½ tsp yellow mustard
- ¼ tsp lemon juice
- 1 drop Tabasco sauce

Directions:

I. Whisk everything together until smooth
II. Store in fridge

Hidden Valley Ranch Dressing

Ingredients:

- 1 C shaken buttermilk
- ¼ C mayonnaise
- 3 T Italian seasoning
- 2 T chives, chopped
- 4 tsp white wine vinegar
- 1 T minced garlic
- ½ tsp salt
- 1/8 tsp pepper to taste

Directions:

I. Add everything into a mason jar or bowl (and pour into jar with a lid) and shake vigorously, and store in fridge

Kraft Thousand Island Dressing

Ingredients:

- ½ C mayo
- 2 T ketchup
- 1 T white wine vinegar
- 2 tsp sugar
- 2 tsp sweet pickle relish
- 1 tsp minced onion
- 1/8 tsp salt and pepper to taste

Directions

I. Add everything together in a mason jar and shake.

II. Store in fridge

Little Caesar's Crazy Sauce

Ingredients:

- 1 can tomato puree
- ½ tsp salt and pepper
- ¼ tsp garlic powder
- ¼ tsp dried basil
- ¼ tsp dried marjoram
- ¼ tsp oregano
- ¼ tsp. ground thyme

Directions:

I. Add everything over heat in a small to medium saucepan and simmer for about 30 minutes or so.

II. Stir often

McDonald's Big Mac Sauce

Ingredients:

- ½ C mayo
- 2 T French dressing
- 4 tsp. sweet pickle relish
- 1 T minced onion
- 1 tsp. white vinegar
- 1 tsp. sugar
- 1/8 tsp. salt

Directions:

I. Add everything into a bowl and stir well, cover and store in fridge for at LEAST an hour

McDonald's Honey Mustard Sauce

Ingredients:

- ½ C brown mustard
- 2 T corn syrup
- 4 tsp mustard powder
- 1 ½ tsp white vinegar
- 1 tsp soy sauce
- 1 ½ tsp sugar
- ¼ tsp. cayenne pepper

Directions:

I. Combine everything together in a bowl and blend well together. Store in an air tight container for at least 4-6 hours- or for best results let sit overnight in fridge

McDonald's Hot Mustard Sauce

Ingredients:

- 5 T mayo
- 2 T honey
- 4 tsp grey pompon
- ½ tsp white vinegar

Directions:

I. Add everything together in a bowl and stir well, store in fridge

McDonald's Sweet and Sour Sauce

Ingredients:

I. ¼ C each preserves
II. 1 /4 C apricot preserves
III. 2 T corn syrup (light)
IV. 5 tsp. white vinegar
V. 1 ½ tsp corn starch
VI. ½ tsp soy sauce
VII. ½ tsp. yellow mustard
VIII. ¼ tsp salt
IX. 1/8 tsp garlic powder
X. 2 T water

Directions:

I. Add everything but the water in your blender and puree
II. Pour into a sauce pan and heat over low to medium heat, add in the water and stir
III. Bring to a quick boil and let boil for 3-5 minutes
IV. Once thickened let sit away from heat and let cool
V. Store in fridge in air tight container

Olive Garden House Dressing

Ingredients:

- 1 pkt. Italian dressing mix
- ¾ C olive oil
- ¼ C+ 2 T white vinegar
- ¼ C water
- ½ tsp sugar
- ½ tsp dried Italian seasoning
- ½ tsp salt and pepper
- ¼ tsp garlic powder

Directions:

I. Add everything in a bowl and whisk together NO CLUMPS,
II. Store in fridge in air tight container

Papa John's Garlic Sauce

Ingredients:

- ¼ lbs. salted butter
- 2 tsp garlic powder
- 1/8 tsp salt

Directions:

I. Add butter over low heat and let melt

II. When foamy get rid of the foam on the top

III. Stir in remaining ingredients and stir until garlic powder dissolves

Pizza Hut Creamy Italian Dressing

Ingredients:

- 2 tsp. dried oregano
- 2 tsp. dried basil
- ½ tsp. dried thyme
- ½ tsp. dried rosemary
- 1 tsp. salt
- ½ tsp. pepper
- ¼ C red wine vinegar
- 1 T lemon juice
- ¼ C mayo
- ¾ C EVOO
- 1/3 C parmesan cheese

Directions:

I. Put all of your dried ingredients into a bowl, stir in the vinegar and lemon juice

II. Wisk in the mayo and olive oil

III. Stir in parmesan cheese

IV. Pour into a mason jar with a lid

V. Shake well

VI. Store in fridge

Ponderosa's Steak Sauce

Ingredients:

- 1/3 C Heinz steak sauce
- 1/3 C Worcestershire sauce
- 1/3 C A1 sauce
- 2 T corn syrup

Directions:

I. Add everything in order listed above and pour into a mason jar with a lid
II. Shake and store in fridge

Red Lobster Tartar Sauce

Ingredients:

- ½ C mayo
- 1 ½ T minced onion
- 1 T sweet pickle relish
- 1 ½ tsp. shredded carrots
- 1 ½ tsp. sugar

Directions:

I. Add everything together in a bowl, store and chill in fridge

Sbarro sauce

Ingredients:

- 2 cans crushed tomatoes
- 1 C cold water
- 4 oz. Romano cheese
- 12 oz. olive oil
- 10 oz. diced onions
- 1 oz. fresh garlic
- ½ oz. Italian parsley
- 3 oz. cooking wine

  Spice
- 2 T salt and pepper
- 2 tsp oregano
- ½ tsp. red pepper flakes
- ½ tsp black pepper
- 2 tsp basil

Directions:

I. Heat the oil in a skillet and sauté the onions and garlic

II. Deglaze with the sherry and parsley

III. Add tomatoes, water, cheese and spices, stir well

IV. Bring to a boil and simmer for about 45 minutes to one hour

Taco Bell Green Sauce

Ingredients:

- 1 lbs. fresh tomatillos
- 3 large jalapeno peppers
- Onion, chopped
- 2 T minced garlic
- Cilantro
- 2 C chicken broth
- 1 T vegetable oil

Directions:

I. Stem the pepper and husk the tomatillos and boil with the peppers n the chicken broth for about 10 minutes

II. Strain

III. Add everything but the oil together and blend until smooth

IV. Reduce heat and cook until thick

Taco Bell Hot Sauce

Ingredients:

- 1 can tomato paste
- 3 C water
- 2 tsp. cayenne pepper
- 1 ½ T chili powder
- 2 ½ tsp salt
- 2 tsp cornstarch
- 2 tsp. white vinegar
- 1 T minced dried onion
- 2 T canned jalapeno slices

Directions:

I. Heat water and sauce over medium heat and stir until smooth

II. Add in the peppers and remaining ingredients Stir until boiling

III. Let stand and pour into fridge save container

T.G.I. Friday's Soy Dressing

Ingredients:

- 1/3 C peanut oil
- 1/3 C cider vinegar
- 1/3 C water
- 2 T soy sauce
- 2 T green onion stems
- 1 T honey
- ½ tsp hot mustard

Directions:

I. Add everything into a jar with a lid and shake well
II. Store in fridge

Wicker's BBQ Sauce

Ingredients:

- 1 ½ C cider vinegar
- 1 tsp. black pepper
- 2 ½ salt
- 1 ½ tsp sugar
- 4 tsp. chili powder
- 1 tsp mustard
- 1 tsp paprika
- ½ tsp ground cumin

Directions:

I. Add everything together to your sauce pan and heat over low to medium heat for about 10 minutes

II. This is a marinade or BBQ braise

Printed in Great Britain
by Amazon

60642365R00020